CIRCUS SKILLS

STEPHANIE TURNBULL

W
FRANKLIN WATTS
LONDON•SYDNEY

 An Appleseed Editions book

First published in 2012 by Franklin Watts
338 Euston Road, London NW1 3BH

Franklin Watts Australia
Hachette Children's Books
Level 17/207 Kent St, Sydney, NSW 2000

© 2012 Appleseed Editions

Created by Appleseed Editions Ltd,
Well House, Friars Hill, Guestling,
East Sussex TN35 4ET

Designed and illustrated by Guy Callaby
Edited by Mary-Jane Wilkins
Photo research by Su Alexander

ISBN 978 1 4451 0982 4

Dewey Classification: 791.3

A CIP catalogue for this book is available from the British Library.

Picture credits
l = left, r = right, t = top, b = bottom, c = centre
Page 2 homydesign/Shutterstock; 3 Fotosutra.com/Shutterstock; 4 Losevsky Pavel/
Shutterstock; 5tl PavleMarjanovic/Shutterstock, bl Hemera/Thinkstock,
r (background) Fotosutra.com/Shutterstock, (main image) ChipPix/Shutterstock;
6 homydesign/Shutterstock; 8 Tamara Kulikova/Shutterstock; 9 (background)
Fotosutra.com/Shutterstock, (main image) Sergey Petrov/Shutterstock;
10 Photodisc/Thinkstock; 12 Aij Lehtonen/Shutterstock; 14 Galina Barskaya/
Shutterstock; 16 Jose Gil/Shutterstock; 17 Guy Callaby; 18 Regien Paassen/
Shutterstock; 19 iStockphoto/Thinkstock; 20 Shutterstock; 21t Katarzyna Krawiec/
Shutterstock, c Tischenko Irina/Shutterstock, bl Spaxiax/Shutterstock, br Akva/
Shutterstock; 22t Nadi555/Shutterstock, bl Noam Armonn/Shutterstock, br AJT/
Shutterstock; 23 Aispix/Shutterstock; 25 Natursports/Shutterstock; 26t Hemera
Technologies/Thinkstock, b Shutterstock; 27t Antonio Petrone/Shutterstock,
b (composite) Thinkstock & Shutterstock; 28t Calstock Unicycle Club/www.
circusintoschools.co.uk, b Digital Vision/Thinkstock; 29 Zoom Team/Shutterstock;
30 Ablestock.com/Thinkstock; 31t (composite) Thinkstock & Shutterstock,
b Shutterstock:

Front cover: Ryan McVay/Thinkstock

Printed in Singapore

Franklin Watts is a division of Hachette Children's Books,
an Hachette UK company.
www.hachette.co.uk

WANT TO JOIN THE CIRCUS?

If you've ever been to see a circus, you'll know how much fun it can be – amazing acrobatics, unbelievable balancing acts and death-defying stunts. There are many circus skills you can learn yourself. This book gives you the facts, tips and tricks you need to start your circus career… or just impress your friends!

HINTS AND WARNINGS

Boxes with a light bulb give handy hints for improving skills.

There's an exclamation mark next to safety warnings and advice.

▲ *Performers wave to the huge crowd at the Old Moscow Circus in Russia.*

4

Why circus skills?

Circus skills are great exercise. They improve balance, flexibility and co-ordination. They train your brain, too – you really need to concentrate when you're juggling balls or spinning plates! Some skills are better practised alone, with no distractions, but others are fun to learn in a group – especially when you need a friend to hold on to!

◀ *Many acrobatic skills involve balancing moving or unstable objects, such as this rolling cylinder.*

Tough stuff

If you want to swing from a trapeze or teeter at the top of a human pyramid, then be patient – these skills take years of professional training. The first step is to learn basic balancing and tumbling skills. Pick skills you enjoy, then practise them a lot. Remember, NEVER attempt anything dangerous.

▼ *Mid-air moves like this take years of practice.*

★ *The first modern circus began in 1768. Philip Astley showed acrobatic horseriding tricks in a circular space. He later added clowns, jugglers, tightrope walkers and performing animals.*

▲ *Child performers from an old circus.*

★ *One of the most famous circuses ever was the Barnum and Bailey Circus, or The Greatest Show on Earth. It had a huge elephant named Jumbo and many odd sideshow acts.*

★ *Many circuses today don't use animals. Acrobats perform with dramatic stage sets. A Canadian company, Cirque du Soleil, once performed an underwater show in an enormous tank!*

STARTING TO JUGGLE

Juggling uses throwing and catching skills that have been part of circuses for hundreds of years. If you want to create your own circus act, juggling is the perfect place to start. It's tricky to learn, so you'll need lots of time and patience… and something to juggle, of course.

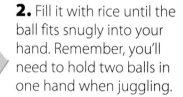

Balls and bean bags

Circus performers juggle with scarves, rings, **clubs** and even knives or flaming torches! As a beginner, all you need are three balls or bean bags. Here's an easy way to make your own juggling balls. They're just as good as bought equipment – and a lot cheaper.

1. Cut the neck off a balloon.

2. Fill it with rice until the ball fits snugly into your hand. Remember, you'll need to hold two balls in one hand when juggling.

3. To seal the ball, cut the neck off another balloon and stretch it over the first, covering the open end.

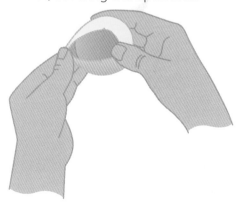

4. Make two more balls and you're ready to juggle!

One ball juggling

First learn to juggle with just one ball to get the throw right.

1. Stand with the ball in your weaker hand (the hand you don't write with). The other hand is your stronger hand. Hold the ball at waist height, close to your body. Toss it in an arc to your stronger hand. Try to make the top of the arc level with your eyes.

2. Throw the ball in the same way from your stronger hand to your weaker hand. Practise until every throw is the same height. Keep them gentle and controlled.

Time for two

Next, take a ball in each hand.

1. Throw the ball from your weaker hand first. As the ball reaches the top of its arc, throw the second ball. Don't worry about catching either – just concentrate on timing the throws. After a while, try catching the balls.

2. Next, try throwing with your stronger hand first.

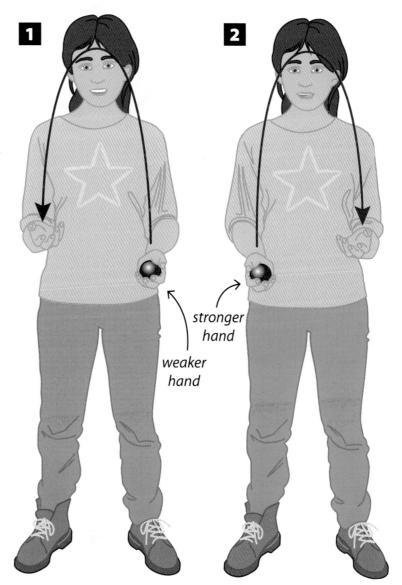

stronger hand

weaker hand

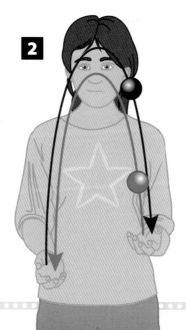

Practise juggling next to your bed. Dropped balls will fall on the bed rather than the floor, so you'll waste less time bending down to pick them up.

When you can throw and catch two balls confidently, turn the page and try juggling with three balls!

MASTERING JUGGLING

Juggling with three balls is very tricky at first, but don't despair. Remember the throwing style you've already learned, follow the steps below and take things slowly. Practise regularly and don't get too frustrated – if it really isn't going well, take a break and try again later!

The third ball

Take two balls in your weaker hand and one ball in your stronger hand. Now spend some time throwing two balls again (see page 7). Although you're not using the third ball yet, you're getting used to having an extra ball in your weaker hand.

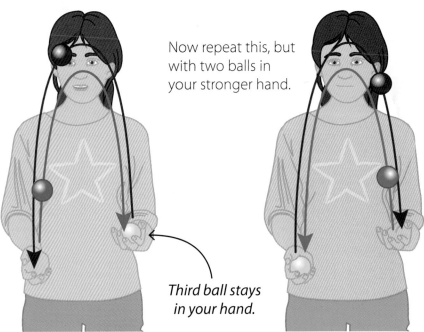

Now repeat this, but with two balls in your stronger hand.

Third ball stays in your hand.

Next, hold two balls in your weaker hand again. Throw the two balls again (from the weaker hand first, then the stronger hand), and as the second ball reaches the top of the arc, throw the third ball from your weaker hand. It doesn't matter where the third ball goes – just try letting it go.

Concentrate on throwing – don't worry about catching anything.

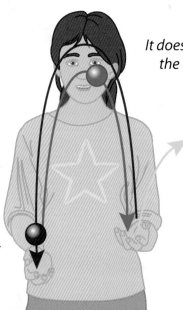

It doesn't matter where the third ball goes.

If you feel confused, go back a few steps or even start again with one ball.

Catching the balls

Practise throwing all three balls, trying to catch the first two. Once you can do this, start throwing the third ball in an arc, like the others. Finally, try catching the third ball too, so you end up with two balls in your stronger hand and one in your weaker hand.

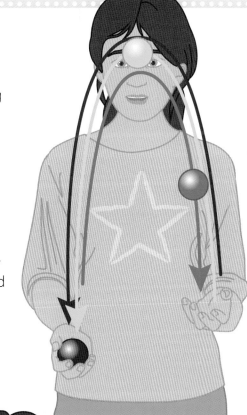

Keep going!

Now you've got all the moves – it's just a case of repeating them! As the third ball peaks, throw the one in your stronger hand back to your weaker hand. Then as that peaks, throw the one in your weaker hand to your stronger hand… and you're juggling.

Keep your hands low and relaxed so you don't snatch at the balls and fling them in all directions.

A juggler with two diabolos.

CLEVER JUGGLING TRICKS

Once you master the juggling action (called a three-ball cascade), try juggling with items such as scarves or clubs. Remember, these props move differently in the air, so you may feel as if you're starting again. You can also stick with the balls and learn a few tricks.

You can juggle with everyday things – but steer clear of precious or breakable items!

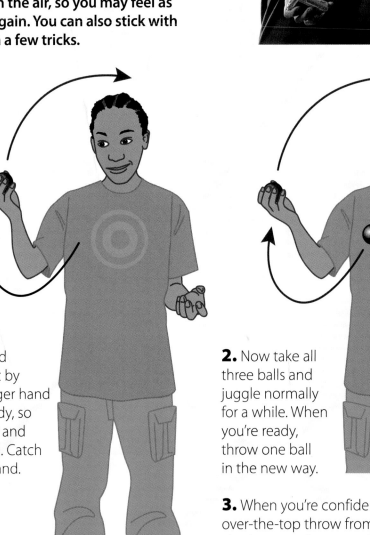

Over the Top
One neat effect is to throw a ball up and over the top of the other balls, instead of inside the previous ball's arc.

1. Take one ball and practise throwing it by moving your stronger hand away from your body, so the ball goes wider and higher than normal. Catch it in your weaker hand.

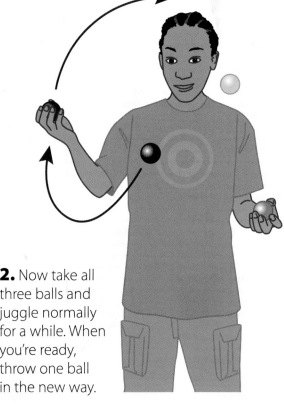

2. Now take all three balls and juggle normally for a while. When you're ready, throw one ball in the new way.

3. When you're confident, learn the over-the-top throw from your weaker hand. This lets you do two over-the-top throws in a row. You could even try throwing over the top every time.

Columns

Another good trick is called Columns, or One Up Two Up.

1. Start with one ball and practise throwing it straight up – not across to your other hand – and catching it.

Don't throw it higher than eye level.

2. Now take two balls in your hand. Throw the first as before. As it peaks, move your hand sharply outwards and throw the second ball up in the same way.

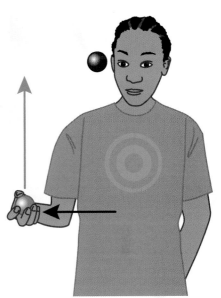

3. Next, move your hand back to catch the first ball and toss it up again. Once you can do this, move your hand out again to catch the second ball and toss it… and keep the pattern going.

4. Take the third ball in your other hand. Throw the first ball up, then the second – but as you throw the second ball, throw the third straight up at exactly the same time.

5. Keep throwing and catching the third ball at the same time as the second. Now the balls look as if they're moving in columns.

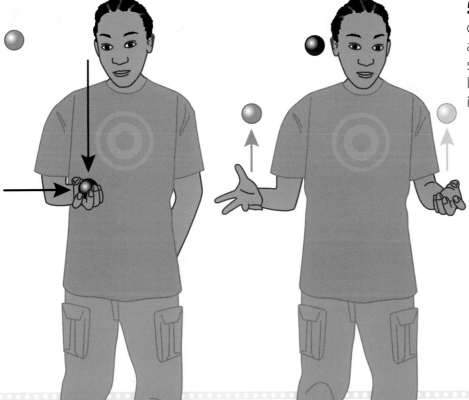

Practise every move with both hands – otherwise you'll become what experts call a lopsided juggler!

PERFECT PLATE SPINNING

Spinning plates is a classic circus act. Performers twirl plates, bowls or other flat objects on sticks which are either held or clipped into upright stands. The more plates they keep going, the more impressive it looks. The world record for the most plates spinning at once is 108.

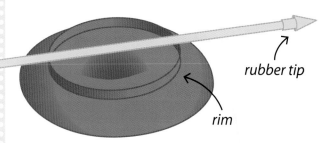

rubber tip

rim

Get the gear

Here's the first rule of plate spinning: don't use real plates. Special plastic plates only cost a few pounds and have a thin rim and slightly domed shape that make them easier to spin. They are usually sold with a rubber-tipped stick.

Start spinning

A plate works like a spinning top – the faster it spins, the more stable it is. The trick is getting it going. It's not too hard, but it does take practice.

1. First, hook the rim of the plate on the stick. Hold the stick straight.

2. Using your wrist (not your whole arm) start moving the stick in small circles, gradually getting faster.

3. The plate will probably fall off the stick at first, but practise until you can keep it on. As you turn the stick faster, the plate straightens up. When it's flat, stop turning the stick and hold it steady.

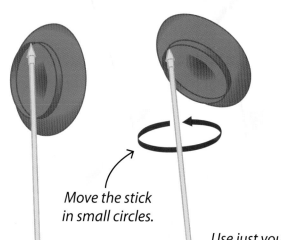

Move the stick in small circles.

Use just your wrist, not your whole arm.

4. The plate should spin smoothly for about 20 to 30 seconds before it slows down. To keep it going, either twirl the stick again, or give the plate a quick, gentle push with your hand.

Cool plate tricks

Once you can spin a plate, try these tricks. Set them to music and you've got your own plate-spinning routine!

Finger Spinner

Get the plate spinning, then carefully move your index finger up the stick. Lift the plate so it's spinning on your finger.

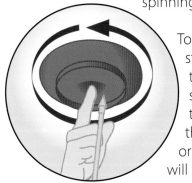

To move it back to the stick, flip it gently into the air and position the stick underneath. As the plate drops, move the stick down a little, or the sudden contact will stop the spinning.

Under the Leg

Hold the stick near the top and steadily move it under your leg. Bring it back up with your other hand.

Three in One Hand

Use the hand you prefer to spin with to get one plate going. Move it to your other hand. Now pick up a second plate and grip it in the hand holding the first plate.

Hook the second stick under the rim of the second plate and start it spinning. Now move it to your other hand, crossing the sticks so you can hold them both.

Start a third plate in the same way and position it between the first two, towards the back. If you're quick, you can even get a fourth plate spinning in your free hand!

Spread all the plates and sticks in front of you.

Why not combine juggling and plate spinning? Hold two juggling balls in one hand while you get your plate spinning in the other. Then juggle the two balls as in steps 1-3 of the Columns trick on page 11.

TAKING A TUMBLE

Circus acts usually include **tumbling** moves such as somersaults and back flips. Acrobats often perform group routines, or balance on each other to create human towers. If you want to be an acrobat, here are a few basic moves you should know.

The safest way of learning acrobatics is from an expert. Always practise on soft gym mats and spend five to ten minutes **warming up** first, to prepare your body for exercise.

▲ *Good gymnasts are fit and strong, and hold poses gracefully.*

Forward Roll

Forward rolls are one of the first and easiest tumbling moves to learn.

1. Squat on a gym mat, like this, with your hands just in front of your feet.

2. Tuck your chin into your chest and lower your head until the back of your neck is touching the floor. As you move forward, straighten your legs a little.

3. Now push off with your feet and roll over, staying curled as you roll…

4. …and finish in a standing position.

Handstand

A handstand is easier to learn if you have someone to hold your legs up. You can also learn against a wall.

1. Stand straight with your arms above you. Now lunge forward like this.

2. Kick your back leg up, then follow with the other leg.

3. Hold your legs as straight as you can.

If you feel you're going to fall forward, move one hand around so your body turns to the side. You can then step back down.

Lead with either leg.

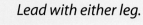

The Chair Move

Once you know some basic moves, you could learn acrobalance, in which two or more people balance on or lift each other. Here's a good position to start with.

1. One person (called the base) stands with knees bent and back straight. The other (called the flyer) stands facing them. Each grasps the other's wrists. This is a **circus grip**.

2. The flyer steps on to the base's knees, pressing down so as not to push away the base.

3. Now both slowly stretch out their arms and lean away from one another.

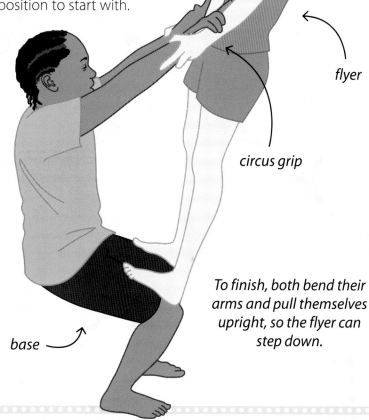

flyer

circus grip

base

To finish, both bend their arms and pull themselves upright, so the flyer can step down.

HULA HOOPING

Many people learn how to hula hoop to keep fit, but it's also a great circus skill. Acrobats perform spectacular displays while twirling hoops around their waist, neck, ankles, arms or legs... or all at once!

Choose a hoop

You need a hoop which is the right size. The hoop should come up to your waist when you stand it in front of you. Larger, heavier hoops are easier to keep moving than small, light ones. Try a few to find one you're comfortable with.

Start spinning

Stand with one foot in front of the other. Hold the hoop against your lower back and give it a big push around your waist.

It doesn't matter which direction you spin the hoop.

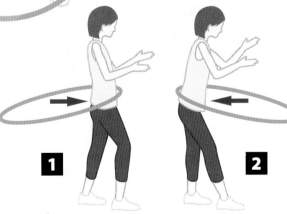

Keep it moving

Keep the hoop moving by shifting your weight from one foot to the other, so you're rocking gently. As the hoop rolls across your front (**1**), shift forward, and as it rolls across your back (**2**), shift backwards. Don't try to move your body in circles.

Once you can keep the hoop moving, try walking while hooping. Take small steps and always move in the direction the hoop is spinning!

Hoop tricks

Try spinning the hoop around different parts of your body. First, get it twirling around your waist. When it's in front of you, dip forward so the hoop starts spinning around your chest…

…then stand up and keep it moving.

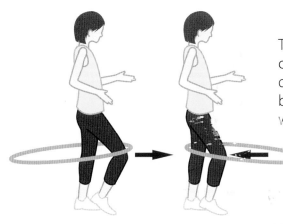

To spin it at knee height, put your weight on one leg and bend the other. Let the hoop move down your body, then twirl it around your knees by rocking the bent leg backwards and forwards with the motion of the hoop.

Try moving your arms in and out of the hoop, or even spinning two hoops at once. Experiment and make up your own moves!

SUPER ★ FACTS

★ Some performers hula hoop with tractor tyres or have fiery spokes around their hoop.

★ Early hoops were made of bamboo or stiff, woven grasses. Now they are usually plastic or light metal.

★ Some Native Americans hoop dance to tell stories. Each dancer uses as many as 30 hoops, interlocking them to form animal and bird shapes.

★ In 2009, American hooper Paul 'Dizzy Hips' Blair spun 132 hoops at once, setting a new world record.

BALANCING SKILLS

Many circus activities rely on balancing skills. The skills on this page need special equipment, so the best place to learn them is in a circus skills class, with a qualified teacher so you don't hurt yourself!

Walking tall

Stilt walkers jump, turn and even dance on high stilts that strap on at the foot, ankle and knee. If you want to learn, start with low, hand-held stilts. Wear a helmet and padding, and have someone (called a spotter) to support you.

► *Striding out on high stilts like this takes great balance and a lot of practice.*

1. Ask your spotter to help you up on the stilts. Get used to standing with your legs straight.

2. Lift each stilt in turn to walk on the spot. Keep your feet firmly on the blocks as you raise each stilt. Next, try taking small steps forward, lifting each stilt high as if you're marching.

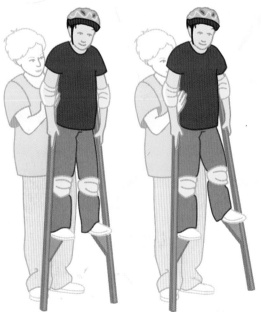

Practise on a soft, non-slip surface.

If you fall off stilts, curve your body inwards. Never fling your hands out to break your fall – you could seriously hurt yourself.

Tightrope walking

Tightrope walking isn't too dangerous... as long as your rope is only a few centimetres off the ground! You can buy special rope that is a thin, flat strip of material. Secure it between two supports, keeping it slack.

Now ask a spotter to help you on to the middle of the rope, where it dips. Bend your knees and stretch out your arms for balance. When you feel steady, try walking forward.

▶ *A tightrope walker practises with a harness for safety.*

Unicycling

Balancing on a one-wheeled bike is a real challenge! You need a spotter to support you, or something to hold on to, such as a handrail.

1. Half sit on the unicycle, like this, with one pedal near the floor. Hold your support.

2. Step on the lower pedal first, then the higher one. The wheel will turn backwards a little. This is different from the way you ride a bike, when you step on the higher pedal first to push the bike forwards.

3. Lean forward slightly and try pedalling. If you're going to fall, let the unicycle go and stay on your feet.

BECOMING A CLOWN

Every circus needs a clown! If you're good at making people laugh and have bags of energy and confidence, clowning is for you. Look at these ideas for creating a clown character, then turn the page to learn **slapstick** skills that will make your clown act a hit.

Clown categories

The most famous type of clown is called the **auguste** clown. Augustes have boldly-painted faces, silly wigs and big red noses. Other performers are whiteface clowns, who have (you guessed it) white faces and less garish features. There are also character clowns, for example comical policemen and sad-faced tramps.

Creative costumes

Don't spend money on an expensive costume – create your own! If you want to be a wacky auguste, search dressing-up boxes and charity shops for wide ties, loud jackets and patterned shirts. For an outfit to look funny, everything should be either big and baggy, or small and tight!

brightly coloured braces

waistcoat too small

trousers too big

dressing gown, or inside-out coat

odd socks

big slippers (stuffed with socks to keep feet in place)

Funny faces

To look like a proper clown, use face paints to give yourself a funny face. Here's how to create a simple clown face, which you can adapt to suit your character. Don't get carried away, though – if you look too grotesque, you may scare your audience!

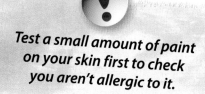

Test a small amount of paint on your skin first to check you aren't allergic to it.

1. Smear white face paint above your eyes and around your mouth, using a make-up sponge or your fingers.

2. With a thin brush, paint the end of your nose red so it looks rounded. Outline your mouth area in red too.

3. Paint your bottom lip red and add little tear-shaped ends to make a smile.

Do this the other way up for a sad face.

4. Paint high eyebrows and add features such as vertical lines above and below your eyes, and stars or freckles on your cheeks.

A sad clown could have a tear instead.

SUPER ★ FACTS

★ Clowns are sometimes called Joeys. They are named after Joseph Grimaldi (1778-1837), a famous English performer who played Clown Joey for years.

★ One of the best-known augustes was a Russian clown called Albert Fratellini (1886-1961). He was the first clown to wear a big red nose.

★ Many film and TV actors use clowning skills, for example Charlie Chaplin, Laurel and Hardy, Jim Carrey and Mr Bean.

CLOWNING AROUND

You look like a clown – now start acting like one! Clown acts are carefully-planned, practised sketches with lots of over-the-top physical comedy. To create your own clown routine, you need some **miming** skills.

For ideas, watch films starring Laurel and Hardy, Charlie Chaplin, Buster Keaton, Harold Lloyd or Jacques Tati. Notice how they use mime and great timing to be funny.

▲ *Buster Keaton (right) with Roscoe Arbuckle, another great mime artist.*

Mime moves

Although your clown could speak in a funny voice, many clowns are silent. Their movements tell the story. The key is to exaggerate everything.

For example, a clown may stub his toe…

…or suddenly realize he's late…

… or need to go to the toilet really badly.

Practise making every action big and bold, and don't rush your moves, otherwise the audience won't have a clue what's going on!

Funny walks

Exaggerate the way your clown walks. If you're a proud, cocky character, take big strides with your nose in the air. If you're timid and easily scared, crouch down and keep peering over your shoulder. Clowns are often clumsy, so try tripping by deliberately catching one foot behind the other ankle as you walk.

◄ *Pretending to slip on a banana skin then tumbling over is a classic clown joke.*

Clown teamwork

It's often easier to be funny if you have another clown to work with. Think of two comical characters – for example, a sleepy policeman and a clever robber, or a strict teacher and a cheeky pupil – and invent a silly story. Plan your moves carefully – if you both trip or fall at the same time, the audience won't know who to look at.

▶ *Plan your costumes together. How about dressing as identical twins, like this duo?*

Fake fights

Here are some moves to help you stage a clown fight. Start by warming up, use gym mats, and practise in slow motion at first.

1. Two clowns face each other. Blue takes a swing at Red's face with the arm nearest the audience – but stops just before she touches him. Red jerks his head to one side, as if hit, and at the same time claps his hands to make the sound of a slap. People will be watching Red's face, so they won't notice the clap.

2. Red staggers backwards. His legs wobble, his eyes roll and he falls back with his legs bent. As he lands, he slaps the ground with both hands to make the sound of the fall.

clap hands

slap hands on the mat

3. Angry, Red stands up and swings a punch. Blue ducks.

4. The force of Red's swing spins him round, making him lose his balance and fall – again.

CLOWN PROPS

Professional clowns use special gimmicks, such as tiny cars, bikes that fall apart or ovens that explode. You can buy many clown props, but it's cheaper to create your own – and they will make your act more original, too.

Get ahead... get a hat

Having fun with one item can be more effective than filling the stage with lots of one-joke props. For example, think of all the things you could do with a hat. It could get stuck on your head and have to be removed with an unscrewing motion… then you could drop it, try to pick it up, and each time accidentally kick it away… then creep up behind it, leap on it – and squash it flat.

Classic props

Everyday items can be just as funny as special props. How about getting wedged in a toddler-sized chair, trying to swat an imaginary fly with a newspaper or becoming tangled in toilet paper?

Mops and buckets of water can be fun, as long as you don't mind getting wet – or having a mop in your face! Use the famous trick of swinging an extra bucket of water over the audience, only to reveal it contains confetti instead.

Fun with foam

Use large sponges or pieces of **foam rubber** to invent outsize props such as a ridiculously big mobile phone, a fake brick or a huge lollipop. You could also make a hole in a sponge and glue in a wooden stick to create a mallet for bopping another clown over the head.

Combining skills

Clowns often use circus props, such as clubs, balls or unicycles to copy serious circus acts. For example, a clown might juggle, but drop balls on his head, or wear high stilts that make him stagger all over the stage. If you know other circus skills, make sure you use them in your clown act!

▶ *This clown is juggling and balancing on a ball at the same time.*

Only use circus skills you've already perfected. For example, don't pretend to wobble out of control on a unicycle unless you're an expert... or your act may end in disaster!

DAREDEVIL STUNTS

Some circus acts are so jaw-droppingly dangerous that you can't believe your eyes. Many use basic skills, such as balancing, but are so hard that they take years of practice – and nerves of steel. Here are a few routines that are NOT for beginners!

Knife throwing

Which would you rather be: a knife thrower hurling weapons at your assistant strapped to a moving wheel – or the assistant, watching helplessly as knives whizz towards you? This act is called the Wheel of Death and is one of the most perilous stunts in the circus.

Try using the idea of knife throwing as part of a clown act. While the terrified assistant stands quaking with eyes shut, the thrower swaps his (plastic) knives for shaving foam pies and pelts the assistant with them.

Mad motorbikes

If the Wheel of Death sounds a little tame, what about the Globe of Death? In this unbelievable routine, motorbike riders zoom around the inside of a large metal cage. At the climax, another person stands in the middle of the cage as the bikers loop and criss-cross around him.

◀ *Stunt riders need great balance, steering and timing skills – and perfect control over their speed.*

★ In 2006, a four year old boy named Maximus Garcia became the youngest recorded Globe of Death motorbike rider.

★ The Great Throwdini performs a version of the Wheel of Death called the Veiled Wheel. In this stunt, a paper screen in front of the moving wheel means he can't see his assistant at all.

★ Extreme sword-swallowing acts include swallowing a sword in a shark tank, being lowered upside down on to a sword, and swallowing a sword while skipping with a rope… on a unicycle.

Swallowing swords

Here's what every sword swallower must remember: don't swallow! The key to this terrifying act is overcoming the urge to gag when something is put down your throat, so that there is a clear passage from the mouth to the stomach. Surprisingly, few sword swallowers suffer fatal injuries… although they often have a sore throat.

▲ Sword swallowers must keep their head back and upper body straight, so the sword slides smoothly down their throat.

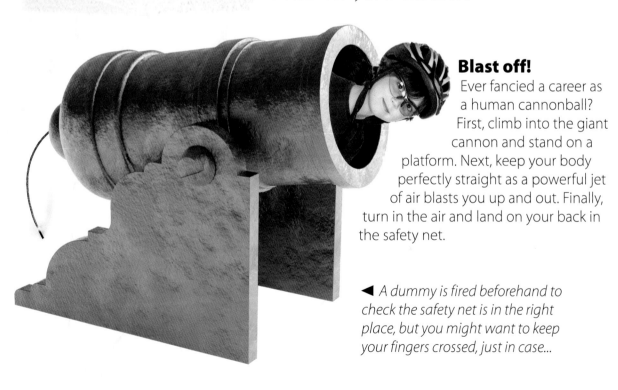

Blast off!

Ever fancied a career as a human cannonball? First, climb into the giant cannon and stand on a platform. Next, keep your body perfectly straight as a powerful jet of air blasts you up and out. Finally, turn in the air and land on your back in the safety net.

◄ A dummy is fired beforehand to check the safety net is in the right place, but you might want to keep your fingers crossed, just in case…

WHAT NEXT?

▲ *Members of a kids' unicycle club in Cornwall meet to practise their unicycling skills.*

Once you've decided which circus skills to learn, the next stage is simple: practise. Some skills, such as juggling or clowning, can be practised at home, outdoors or at school. Others, such as unicycling or tumbling, need places with gym mats and expert help.

Classes and workshops

There are many circus classes and workshops across the UK. Online resources such as the Youth Circus Workshop database (see page 31) list what's on in your area. If you're interested in joining the circus after you leave school, you can apply for circus skills courses at colleges.

Putting on a show

Circus stars need confidence to perform in front of big audiences, so try staging small shows at school or parties. Plan your act carefully and make sure you have all the props you need. Keep people entertained by making jokes or getting volunteers to help.

▼ *Watch entertainers at children's parties to get ideas for your own performance.*

Expand your skills

Think about other hobbies that will improve your circus skills, such as dance, gymnastics, martial arts or acting. If you enjoy performing, how about learning how to make costumes, apply stage make-up or do magic tricks? Look out for other *Super Skills* books for ideas!

Including a few magic tricks in your act is a great way of grabbing attention.

▼ *Ringmasters need to be outgoing people who keep the show moving and can deal with unexpected events.*

Circus careers

Acrobats and clowns aren't the only people who work in a circus. There are **set designers**, **choreographers** and all kinds of technicians controlling music, lighting and machinery. And don't forget the ringmaster, who introduces acts, entertains the audience and works hard to promote the circus.

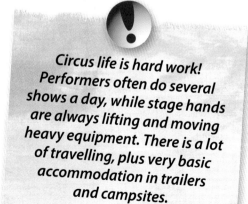

Circus life is hard work! Performers often do several shows a day, while stage hands are always lifting and moving heavy equipment. There is a lot of travelling, plus very basic accommodation in trailers and campsites.

GLOSSARY

auguste
A type of clown with exaggerated make-up, who is traditionally a clumsy, friendly joker. There are many different stories about how augustes got their name, but it may come from German slang meaning 'fool'.

choreographer
Someone who creates dance steps and arranges them into patterns and sequences for dances.

circus grip
A way for two acrobats to hold hands securely. Each grabs the other's wrists, which makes it hard to lose their grip and let go.

club
A stick, usually about 50 cm long and made of plastic, that is shaped a bit like a bowling pin – narrow at one end (where it is held) and wider and heavier at the other end.

foam rubber
A spongy material that is often used for padding in cushions and furniture.

gimmick
A specially-designed prop with a trick part, such as a hidden spring or a secret mechanism, that makes something unexpected happen.

miming
Showing actions, emotions or character through gestures, expressions and movements instead of words.

set designer
Someone who creates stage scenery and props. A good set design should look impressive, but not distract attention from performers.

sideshow
A small show that takes place alongside the main circus. Traditionally, sideshows feature bizarre or dangerous acts such as sword swallowing or fire breathing.

slapstick
Comedy that is silly, funny and over the top.

tumbling
Gymnastics, such as rolls, leaps and somersaults, performed without any special equipment.

warming up
Preparing your body for exercise. Warms-ups include marching or running on the spot, bouncing on your toes, jumping and gentle stretches.

USEFUL WEBSITES

www.cirquedusoleil.com
Learn more about this famous circus company and watch clips of their amazing acrobatic shows.

www.circusarts.org.uk/i-want-to/learn-circus-skills/index.php
Find all kinds of circus-related information, including a link to the Youth Circus Workshop database, where you can check circus classes and groups in your local area.

www.jugglingworld.biz/index.php?/Juggling-Tricks/spinning-plate-tricks.html
Watch a very useful video demonstrating how to spin a plate and do the tricks shown in this book.

www.monkeysee.com/search?term=juggling
Learn basic juggling skills and new tricks using these helpful video tutorials.

www.acrobalance.org/wiki/index.php/Category:Beginner
Find lots of graceful acrobalance moves that are suitable for beginners.

www.hulahooping.com
Discover pretty much everything there is to know about hula hoops, including the history of hooping, tips to improve your skills, and information about how hooping can help keep you fit and healthy.

www.circusintoschools.co.uk
Read about a circus company that runs all kinds of circus skills workshops in schools.

INDEX